Copy editor: My-Trang Nguyen
Graphic designer: Anne Bérubé
Scanner operator: Mélanie Sabourin

E6 Colour development: Laboratoire Sel d'argent

P. 176-177: An Urban Frescoe
  Concept and design: © Cité de la création
  Co-producers: Commission de la capitale nationale du Québec et Société
  de développement des entreprises culturelles du Québec (SODEC)

P. 193: Still photograph from the set of *The Baroness and The Pig,*
a Media Principia production

Canadian Cataloguing-in-Publication Data

Huot, Claudel
    Québec: City of Light

    1. Québec (Quebec) - Pictorial works.   2. Québec (Quebec).
I. Lessard, Michel.   II. Title.

FC2946.37.H8613 2001   971.4'471'00222   C2001-940243-0
F1054.5.Q3H8613 2001

The publisher gratefully acknowledges the support of the Société de
développement des entreprises culturelles du Québec for its publishing program.

We acknowledge the financial support of the Government of Canada through
the Book Publishing Industry Development Program (BPIDP) for our publishing
activities.

© 2001, Les Éditions de l'Homme,
a division of the Sogides Group

Legal deposit: second quarter 2001
Bibliothèque nationale du Québec

ISBN 2-7619-1643-3

EXCLUSIVE DISTRIBUTORS:

• For Canada and the United States:
MESSAGERIES ADP*
955 Amherst St.
Montréal, Quebec
H2L 3K4
Tel.: (514) 523-1182
Fax: (514) 939-0406
* A subsidiary of Sogides Ltée

• For France and other countries:
HAVAS SERVICES
Immeuble Paryseine, 3 Allée de la Seine
94854 Ivry Cedex
Tel.: 01 49 59 11 89/91
Fax: 01 49 59 11 96
Orders: Tel.: 02 38 32 71 00
                Fax: 02 38 32 71 28

• For Switzerland:
DIFFUSION: HAVAS SERVICES SUISSE
P.O. Box 69 - 1701 Fribourg, Switzerland
Tel.: (41-26) 460-80-60
Fax: (41-26) 460-80-68
Internet: www.havas.ch
E-mail: office@havas.ch
DISTRIBUTION: OLF SA
Z.I. 3 Corminbœuf
P.O. Box 1061
CH-1701 FRIBOURG
Orders: Tel.: (41-26) 467-53-33
                Fax: (41-26) 467-54-66

• For Belgium and
  Luxembourg:
PRESSES DE BELGIQUE S.A.
Boulevard de l'Europe 117
B-1301 Wavre
Tel.: (010) 42-03-20
Fax: (010) 41-20-24

For more information about our publications,
please visit our website: **www.edhomme.com**
Other sites of interest: www.edjour.com • www.edtypo.com
www.edvlb.com • www.edhexagone.com • www.edutilis.com

QUÉBEC

CITY OF LIGHT

QUÉBEC
CITY OF LIGHT

Photographs by CLAUDEL HUOT
Text by MICHEL LESSARD

Translated by My-Trang Nguyen

LES ÉDITIONS DE L'HOMME

For my father,
and my beloved family

*T*his *book pays tribute to Old Québec – the Latin Quarter, the Upper Town, Place Royale, rue du Petit-Champlain, rues Saint-Paul and Cartier, the Old Port – and to one of the most beautiful views, along the shore of a magnificent river, that I've ever known. It's where I have chosen to live.*

I salute all those who've also lived, no matter how briefly, within the old walls of this captivating city – friends, lovers, acquaintances.

I dedicate this book to everyone who has shared the unique quality of life in Old Québec; to future decision-makers who, I hope, will protect this World Heritage gem and help preserve its beauty, its special light.

I invite visitors to leave their cars outside the walls, and explore the sites on foot. In this way, you'll get to know and appreciate them better. Welcome to all! I'm convinced that you will come back some day.

Québec, je t'aime!

CLAUDEL HUOT

FROM WHATEVER POINT OF VIEW WE CONSIDER IT, THE CHIEF FEATURE OF QUÉBEC IS ITS PICTURESQUE BEAUTY. BUT ITS SITUATION IS SUCH THAT IT IS IMPOSSIBLE TO TAKE IT IN WHOLLY AT A GLANCE. NO ARTIST COULD PAINT IT IN A SINGLE PICTURE; AND A WHOLE SERIES WOULD FILL A GALLERY OF THE PICTURESQUE, UNDER ALL ITS FORMS; YET IT WOULD STILL BE AN INCOMPLETE PICTURE OF THIS REMARKABLE CITY.

IN ORDER FULLY TO APPRECIATE QUÉBEC'S BEAUTY, AND ITS DIVERSE VARIETY, IT IS INDISPENSABLE THAT WE SHOULD MAKE A TOUR — NOT ONCE ONLY, BUT SEVERAL TIMES. THE TOURIST SHOULD APPROACH IT FROM THE EAST AND THE WEST, BY LAND AND BY WATER, FROM THE NORTH AND FROM THE SOUTH; HE SHOULD LEAVE IT, THEN RETURN, NOW BY ONE ENTRANCE, AGAIN BY ANOTHER; HE SHOULD EXPLORE ITS STREETS, SOMETIMES DRIVING, BUT MORE USEFULLY ON FOOT, STOPPING AT THE CORNERS, GLANCING AT THE CROSS STREETS, FOR ALL ARE AS SO MANY DOORS DISCLOSING NEW PERSPECTIVES, SOME ON THE COUNTRY, OTHERS ACROSS THE RIVER; HERE, OVER THE SUBURBS, OR THE WHARVES; THERE, OVER THE VALLEYS AND SURROUNDING MOUNTAINS.

HE MUST LINGER NEAR THE OLD WALLS, AND LET THEM SPEAK, STROLL THROUGH THE PUBLIC PLACES, THE GARDENS, AND THE INCOMPARABLE DUFFERIN TERRACE. IT IS HERE, ABOVE ALL, THAT HIS ARCHAEOLOGICAL OR SENTIMENTAL PROMENADE SHOULD BEGIN, AND END; THIS IS THE APPROPRIATE SPOT FOR ANYONE WHO LONGS TO SOAR IN THE REGIONS OF POETRY AND INSPIRATION, DREAMING OF THE GREAT EPISODES THAT ARE FOREVER ASSOCIATED WITH THIS ANCIENT CITY.

HERE, THE TOURIST IS CAPTIVATED BY THE UNKNOWN CHARM, WAFTED ON THE AIR BY EVENING BREEZES. THIS ENCHANTMENT IS IRRESISTIBLE, AND THE LONGER HE REMAINS IN QUÉBEC, THE MORE POWERFUL IT GROWS.

HE WHO HAS KNOWN AND LOVED QUÉBEC, NEVER FORGETS IT. THE CHARACTERS OF THE OLD CITY BECOME ENGRAVED IN HIS MEMORY, LIKE PRINT ON PAPER. NOTHING CAN EFFACE THESE IMPRESSIONS, AND THEY REMAIN SO DISTINCT, THAT HE CAN NEVER CONFUSE THEM WITH THOSE OF ANY OTHER CITY.

ADOLPHE-BASILE ROUTHIER
Quebec at the Dawn of the 20th Century, 1900

Very rarely do we find that the picturesque is the work of Art alone; in this particular form of beauty, nature is the great artist. Without compass, chisel or brush, she builds, carves and paints, at every step, marvellous works of beauty.

For a city which is the work of man, to strike the artist's imagination, nature must first come to its aid, and give it waters to bathe its shores, mountains and soaring heights to serve as a fitting background.

Only cities built on the shores of the sea, by a river, or great lake, or at least on a prominent elevation, can be termed picturesque.

A mountain is to a city what a pedestal is to a statue; it is necessary for the setting of the picture.

Great waters serve it as a mirror; they purify, irrigate, and give it life, movement, and a vast variety of aspects. [...]

The city of Québec is, in this respect, the spoiled child of nature.

Adolphe-Basile Routhier
Quebec at the Dawn of the 20th Century, 1900

The king's bastion, seen from the St. Lawrence, c. 1890

FROM THE TOP OF THE BREAKNECK STEPS (*L'ESCALIER* CASSE-COU), THE VIEW IS RAVISHING, especially during the holiday season. Coming down on a snowy evening, the stroller has the impression of taking a trip back in time: *rue du* Petit-Champlain, illuminated by gaily decorated shopwindows, exudes the charm of a French provincial town, that belies an entirely North American way of life.

Among the many images that Québec City offers, one can never be forgotten: the panoramic view that you see as you bicycle along the South Shore, or cross the river. To experience the sweeping vista from the Musée du Québec on the Plains of Abraham to the Musée de la civilisation in the Old Port – which accounts for four centuries of glorious history – is sheer delight.

Ever since 1608, the year Samuel de Champlain set out from the French town of Saintonge, and chose Québec – in the name of the King of France – as a colonial outpost in North America, the ancient capital of New France has been celebrated by artists and writers. The cluster of buildings at the foot of Cap Diamant and along the promontory deploys its charms to enrapt visitors who arrive from the St. Lawrence, a river which acted as a lifeline for the new country and its francophone capital. In Amerindian language, Québec means strait, or narrowness, and refers to the narrowing of the waters at the point where the city itself was built. This strategic passage would be fortified over and over again to control access to the North American continent, until it was dubbed the "Gibraltar of North America" in the 19th century.

Once past the western end of the isle of Orléans, the visitor will be treated to a breathtaking panorama, encompassing valleys, shores, escarpments, mountains and bodies of water in a palette of ever-changing colour, from hour to hour, season to season. Québec is never still. One must live there, or observe it from the heights of Lévis, to confirm the constant and dazzling change.

Québec is incontestably one of the loveliest cities in the world. One has only to see her outline silhouetted against the winter sky, against the extraordinary sunsets, bathed by glowing ice floes; or in summer, crowded and bursting with life, beribboned by *fleurs-de-lys* on Saint-Jean Baptiste Day or during the summer festival. Its cannon batteries pointing in every direction, its soil strewn with vaults, its old grey stones lending a historic texture to the streets, the arrow-like steeples, all are features that set French-speaking America's capital apart from any other.

Recognizing the city of Champlain's unique character, UNESCO placed it on its official listing of World Heritage Sites in 1985, in company with Florence and Istanbul. The United Nations agency said, in part, that "Québec's historic district, including the citadel, the Upper City defended by its bastioned walls and the Lower City with its harbour and old quarter, provides us with an eminent example of a fortified colonial town, which is by far the most complete in North America. […] The former capital of New France, Québec illustrates one of the major stages in population and growth of the Americas during the modern and contemporary period."

Champlain's city has been portrayed in various mediums and styles. Before the advent of photography, many artists used drawings, watercolours, and oils to express their feelings, lingering over the special skyline of this fortified acropolis. The old maps reveal the topographic characteristics of the site, but also its architectural components – images that were sometimes reconstituted by artists from written accounts. The 17th-century map of America by Jean-Baptiste Franquelin, dated 1688, is a good example of this kind of representation, one that lavishly embellishes the site by means of a polychrome rendering, and is not without some documentary value.

After 1763, under the English regime, the city's image took on a new appearance, based on English topographical art. Typical of this genre were the works of James William Peachey (act. 1773-1797) and George Heriot (1766-1844). But James Pattison Cockburn (1779-1847), a British officer, favoured urban scenes instead, depicted through the seasons of the year. Streets, public places, buildings, military structures inside the walled and crenellated city thus became the indelible symbols of Québec. Soon, some 20 painters and pen-and-ink artists of the neo-classic school followed suit, among them were Philip James Bainbrigge (1807-1881), William Wallace (1807-1854), William Henry Bartlett (1809-1854) and Coke Smyth (1808-1867).

QUÉBEC – PHOTOGENIC CAPITAL

In the second half of the 19th century, Joseph Légaré (1795-1855), Cornelius Krieghoff (1815-1872), Lucius O'Brien (1832-1899), Henry Bunnett (1845-1910) and Albert Bierstadt (1830-1902), were attracted by the city's exotic feel and in their turn produced exceptional works in the style of the day. The majority of these colonialist-artists were British, and for them Québec seemed like a jewel in the crown of the new Canadian Confederation, in addition to being a military trophy symbolizing the good relations between two nations.

Local engravers, and some from overseas, also got into the act, depicting the charms of the old city in their own way. Their works were mainly published in tourist guidebooks and illustrated periodicals. In 1860, the visit of the Prince of Wales coincided with the centennial celebrations of the victory on the Plains of Abraham. It was a golden opportunity to "broadcast" images of Québec worldwide. And so they were, countless panoramic views showing Cap Diamant rising above a river swarming with ships adorned with flags suited to the occasion. The *Canadian Illustrated News*, a Montréal weekly launched in 1869, followed a few months later by its French-language edition, *L'opinion publique*, printed drawings of the "old capital" for 13 consecutive years, thus contributing to the city's stereotyped image. In 1888, renowned engravers produced stunning images of Québec in *Artistic Quebec Described by Pen and Pencil*, a book containing unusual renderings of Canadian landscapes.

In the 20th century, the country's most talented artists also paid tribute to Québec. James Wilson Morrice (1865-1924), Charles Huot (1855-1930), Maurice Cullen (1866-1934), Clarence Gagnon (1881-1932), Simone Hudon (1905-1984), Robert Wakeham Pilot (1898-1967), Albert Rousseau (1908-1967), Jean Benoit (born in 1922), Francesco Iacurto (born in 1908), Frederick B. Taylor (1905-1987), Jean-Paul Lemieux (1904-1990), André Garand (born in 1923), Benoit Côté (born in 1929), Betty Baldwin (1889-1981), Claude Picher (1927-1998), Antoine Dumas (born in 1932) and many others have left us works that clearly illustrate their singular perceptions of the city and its light. Added to this illustrious group are lesser-known painters and draughtsmen who today crowd the *rue du* Trésor and other galleries in the Lower Town, conferring on the ancient capital of New France the bohemian look and feel of Montmartre.

The advent of photography allowed Québec to be seen in all its variousness, enshrining the city's views forever. Beginning in the mid-19th century, tourism developed as photography – whose basic techniques were discovered in the 1830s and '40s – became more popular. Times were good, and people who could afford to travel were now interested in taking home mementos of their trips. In 1858, Samuel McLaughlin (1826-1914) offered the first pictures of the capital – dazzling images printed on albuminous paper, while Isai Benoit de Livernois began photographing

Montcalm marketplace, at Saint-Jean Gate, c. 1890

the city – an enterprise that was to span three generations of his family. By the end of the 1850s, pictures were commercially produced in two formats – the visiting card and the stereoscopic card. Both took the world by storm. The former was designed mainly for portraits, but many Québec photographers also used it for landscapes and the recording of particular events. The stereoscopic card – wildly popular between 1860 and 1930 – generated a brisk business that quickly attracted foreign publishers anxious to cream off the best from the local market. Québec, which had a reputation as a city worth discovering for its exotic character, was a favourite subject in both formats. For the first time, views of the city were systematically recorded. Prestigious studios dominated this market – the Livernois family, who remained in business until 1974; George William Ellisson, whose studio was bought in the late 1860s by Louis Prudent Vallée; and William Notman, of Montréal.

This flourishing period also perpetuated visual stereotypes of Champlain's city. Today, traditional architecture, historic monuments, fortifications, industrial landscapes along the shore of the St. Lawrence, winter scenes, public markets and picturesque nature views, are the principal subject matter that mobilize the brotherhood of artists of light. At the turn of the 20th century, as the city was getting ready to celebrate its 300th birthday, the golden age of the

Interior courtyard, Québec Seminary, c. 1880

illustrated postcard heralded a new era. Henceforth, the most exciting scenic views would be immortalized in this format. Around the world, the craze caught on like wildfire. At the major studios – Livernois, Vallée and Notman – favourite shots were converted and offered in postcard form. Scores of publishers in the city and in the rest of Quebec got into the act by launching their own series depicting the "Gibraltar of North America," dominated by that famous Canadian Pacific hotel, the Château Frontenac. Competition was fierce, made worse by the arrival of yet more publishers, from Ontario, the United States, France and Great Britain – a fascinating case of artistic/commercial pursuit that eventually became the subject of a study by art historian Jacques Poitras.

Soon though, makers of stereoscopic cards in Ontario and the United States joined forces with local and national postcard publishers. The years 1907 and 1908 were marked by an unprecedented production of pictures of Québec – its streets, quays, parks, public places, promenades, the Old Port, and especially, Dufferin Terrace – all crowded with feminine silhouettes in long, flowing dresses pushing prams, or with young couples, dressed in the latest Paris fashions. Many of these images were hand-coloured.

We are indebted to the Thaddée Lebel (1872-1946) Funds and the estate of William Bertrand Edwards (1880-1944), for providing us with a generous overview of photographs taken between the two world wars. William Bertrand Edwards was a studio professional who specialized in panoramic and aerial views as well as news photography. He also produced quality reproductions of photographs of the historic city taken by artists who had preceded him. The Thaddée Lebel collection is housed at the Québec Archives.

Since the 1950s, more and more photographers have devoted their art to their private passions, and many among them now work for the bustling and lucrative tourism industry. Never before have the views of Québec been so handsomely served. Each artist has his own style: Pierre Lahoud specializes in aerial views; Denis Tremblay in panoramic takes; Marco Labrecque in urban scenes; the late François Lafortune in intimate black-and-white close-ups. As for Claudel Huot, the drive to interpret Québec's "soul" is a lifetime's challenge.

CLAUDEL HUOT
Photographer

I have been photographing Québec for more than 30 years – pursuing its light and movement, studying its atmosphere, capturing a story on film – at times spending the greater part of a day waiting for that perfect light. A photographer is an artist of light and weather, as disciples of those early 19th-century pioneers, Louis Daguerre and Fox Talbot, are fond of saying, and his palette is governed by the whims of the sun. My own colour scheme plays with a 400-year-old city, built on the shores of a magnificent river, surrounded by mountains, one of the most breathtakingly beautiful views in the world.

I've always loved images. When I was a little boy, our house was filled with illustrated encyclopedias. For my 14th birthday, my godfather gave me my first camera, a Kodak Brownie. It was then that I began leafing through glossy magazines and photography books for beginners.

In 1969, I started to "hang out" in Old Québec, which was then in turmoil. It was a time of student unrest and social upheaval. Around the globe, young people rose up and made themselves seen and heard. Days and nights spent lounging in cafés and bars were cool, and suited me perfectly. It was at Baudelaire – later called Chava-Chava – Chanteauteuil, Nostradamus, bar Élite, Chez Temporel, that I learned to "tame the soul" of Old Québec, at the same time "discovering" what life was all about.

My first professional job took place in a poster shop in Old Québec. There, we made portraits of customers, which we enlarged and reproduced in poster size. I worked with a huge Graflex. The stint did not last long. For my efforts, I received a paper dryer, which I swapped for a Yashica, my first ever camera worthy of the name. I then held a series of odd jobs, in construction, restaurants, hotels, arts and crafts. I lived in a commune in the Saint-Jean Baptiste quarter, devoting money and soul to photography. I even bought my film at the famed Livernois studio!

In 1973, I set up house in a spacious seven-room flat in Lévis, next to the ferryboats and Gosselin, my second photo-supplier. But I simply couldn't photograph Québec from there. Within 10 minutes, I was in Place Royale, hardly able to contain my happiness.

Still life against a frosted window. Hand-coloured, this study was set at 4 X 5 with an old Graflex. (Lévis 1975)

Dauphine Redoubt. Duo tone-coloured print. The shot was made with an old bellows camera 2 1/4 X 3 1/4, whose rangefinder was non-adjustable (1978-1979).

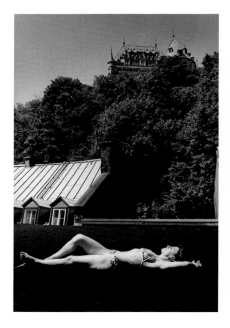 

My neighbour, sunning on the roof. An example of a partially hand-coloured black-and-white photo (1998).
Rue Laval in Old Québec. Nocturnal lighting for the film *Dernier voyage*, directed by Yves Simoneau (mid 1970s).

I've always loved taking portraits, and my studio-apartment had had its share of sitters parading through the door. To explore the light and the way it plays on the bodies of beautiful women is a delightful pursuit. I took a course on dark-room techniques at the Wilbrod-Bhérer school, and processed my own black-and-white film. I also learned how to colour my pictures by hand, the way it was done in the early 20th century. I still use the technique from time to time.

I honed my studio work with seasoned people, especially in the theatre and film businesses. The Quebec film-maker Yves Simoneau, whom I had met at Café Chez Temporel, hired me as a still photographer for his first movie – which was never released – and for other productions: *Le dernier voyage, Les yeux rouges, Dans le ventre du dragon*. I learned a great deal from lighting cameramen, directors of photography and film directors. They are the true masters as far as I'm concerned.

During a stay in France, I had a chance to work on a documentary about cartoons. Later, I polished my skills as a portrait photographer and learned more about shooting stills and exteriors. In the mid-1980s, I began working with Robert Lepage on his stage and movie productions. The collaboration lasted seven years. Lepage is an exceptional lighting expert. For those willing to learn, there is no better teacher. In 1988, I was voted Best Still Photographer of the Year by *Les rendez-vous annuels du cinéma québécois*.

For the past 14 years, I've lived at the foot of Cap Diamant, on *rue du* Petit-Champlain – at the heart of the action. My windows overlook the St. Lawrence River and Lévis. I awake before dawn, and set out with my dog, Céleste, to take advantage of the quality of the light. At dawn, the city belongs to me. In the fall, the colours are

simply dazzling. But it's in winter that my heart skips a beat. There are days when, after a snowstorm, I want to be everywhere at once, just to see how certain spots have been transformed. And I have to move fast, because the moment doesn't last long. It's usually over in a couple of hours.

Roaming through Old Québec, I often meet other photographers at work. I've always admired the work of the late François Lafortune, a master in black-and-white, and that of Claire Dufour, Marco Labrecque, Roger Côté and Eugène Kedl. I'm impressed by their sensitivity, by their original takes on our city.

I can do other kinds of photography, but capturing Old Québec on film is what keeps me going. I'm always looking for new angles from which to view the city. It's a very touristy place and I'm always finding new ways to deal with cars, buses, and the various commercial advertising on billboards and café umbrellas. Because of my work – shooting for postcard companies as well as commissions for private customers, publishers and institutions – I must follow the rhythm of my city. If my impulses are focussed on Old Québec and the Lower Town, I still managed to discover other neighbourhoods, other facets of a city that looks fabulous wherever one goes.

For the past few years, in fact, Québec has become even more beautiful. Mayor Jean-Paul L'Allier has managed to reverse many of the mistakes made by his predecessors. René-Lévesque Boulevard is now rid of its own "Berlin Wall" which overshadowed Parliament Hill. New fountains grace public places, which come alive in winter thanks to brightly lighted fir trees. Streets are adorned with flowers, parks proliferate, the birds are back, and the river will soon be "returned" to the citizens, if only the unscrupulous tour operators can be reined in. A new spirit is taking hold in the city. One should encourage it and support all those who are committed to it. I do my part with my pictures.

I will always be a photographer. I'm 52, and perhaps it's time to visit other parts of the country and the continent. I love nature; watery landscapes like those in Mingan and along the North Shore; and the light in the Far North. Such adventures appeal to me, and perhaps they will help me see Québec even more clearly upon my return.

Michel Lessard interviewed Claudel Huot in Lévis, December 2000

Portrait of the late Jean Millette in the 1988 film *Dans le ventre du dragon* directed by Yves Simoneau.
Portrait of Marie Pier, one of my studio subjects. Precious moments with glamorous women (1986-1988).

With the Passing Days and Seasons

THE LIGHTS OF QUÉBEC

With the passing days and seasons

THE LIGHTS OF QUÉBEC

WHEN NIGHT COMES, EVERYBODY KNOWS WHAT TAKES PLACE IN THE MERRY WORLD WHERE PEOPLE ARE SUPPOSED TO BE AMUSED OR ... BORED. THE GREAT LADIES ARRAY THEMSELVES IN THEIR RICHEST GOWNS, FOR DINNERS, THEATRES OR BALLS. THEY ARE CLOTHED IN SILKS AND LACES, AND PRECIOUS STONES SPARKLE IN THEIR HAIR, ON THEIR NECKS, BOSOMS AND EARS.

WELL! IN SUMMER, QUÉBEC ASSUMES THE APPEARANCE OF THESE GRAND LADIES AND AT NIGHT REALLY PRESENTS A MOST ADMIRABLE VIEW, WHEN THE INCANDESCENT RAYS OF MONTMORENCY'S ELECTRIC SUN FALL UPON THE CITY.

THOUSANDS OF LUMINOUS CLUSTERS HOVER ABOVE IT. SCINTILLATING STARS CROWN ITS HEAD AND ENCIRCLE ITS NECK, AS THOUGH WITH A TIARA OF DIAMONDS, AND ITS MASSIVE WALLS APPEAR AS IF INLAID WITH DIADEMS OF DAZZLING BRILLIANCY.

IT'S NO LONGER A WARLIKE CITY BUT A CITY OF LIGHT, THE CELESTIAL CITY, WITH ITS CONSTELLATIONS SO GROUPED AS TO PRESENT THE PICTURE IN ALL ITS PROUD BEAUTY.

ADOLPHE-BASILE ROUTHIER
Quebec at the Dawn of the 20th Century, 1900

Light and shade on Dufferin Terrace

WHAT A MAGNIFICENT VOLUME BY THE WRITER-JURIST SIR ADOLPHE-BASILE ROUTHIER (1830-1920) – *Quebec at the Dawn of the 20th Century* – published exactly 101 years ago. The author of the lyrics for *O Canada* gave free rein to his whimsical and grandiloquent pen as he put his feelings about his beloved historic capital into words. Judge Routhier's text, printed on glossy paper with an array of typographical flourishes, is accompanied by charming pen-and-ink drawings and photographs from the famous Jules Livernois studio in Québec. It has no peer as the most beautiful book ever produced about the city of Samuel de Champlain. In a lively style, the jurist describes the most significant moments in the capital's history – a site where "the very stones can speak," augmented by eloquent passages describing its landscape and scenery.

Long before Québec was officially recognized as a World Heritage Site, the sophisticated traveller came to appreciate the city's treasures. At the dawn of a new century and millennium, just a few years before celebrating the city's fourth centenary, it's a good time to revisit – in fact, commemorate – Routhier's eloquent vision of the city by reproducing his own words as introductions to each chapter of this book.

Routhier clearly understood the special aura of light around Québec and rendered it elegantly in his prose. Today, the photographer Claudel Huot, who has patrolled the city day-in and day-out for the past 30 years, employs visual images to express the emotions aroused by nature and the urban landscape.

A foggy evening in October on *rue* Saint-Louis

"All photographers become excited by light, that impalpable ingredient which is at the essence of an image," says Huot. "Light inspires, and breathes life into all visual artists. It motivates us to get outside, and sets our creative juices going. Light propels me from my apartment in Old Québec every day, cajoles me into looking through the window for that magical luminous moment."

In Québec, the ever-present river confers exceptional qualities on the light. At times, the water which frames the landscape thickens the air, giving it a special texture.

"I love looking at Québec in all four seasons," Huot adds. "I'm happy to live in a place that is so naturally and inevitably punctuated by these great episodes of nature, regularly returning every year, as astonishing as so many other dramatic changes. This sort of renewal fills life with unexpected surprises. I would be bored by a sky that is always blue, even if it were the purest blue in the whole world."

You need only spread out Claudel Huot's slides over a light table to see how infinitely variable his subject can be, when captured at different times of the day.

Reflections on calm waters, duo-tone and hand-coloured

"My job is to follow the light. From dawn to 9 or 10 a.m., I work nonstop. I'm open to everything: movement, light, the sense of things – animate or inanimate. At 10 o'clock, the light loses its effect, for by that time, the sunlight lacks brilliance. I start work again in the late afternoon. All photographers prefer morning light, and that at the end of day. Both give even the most insignificant things a kind of soul. Dusk, the 'blue hour,' is a magical moment. The mixture of natural and artificial light has something mysterious about it."

For some years now, looking forward to the new millennium and the upcoming celebrations of the city's 400th birthday, the National Commission of the provincial capital has undertaken a vast program of public works, sparing no major buildings. In addition, the city already offers an exceptional *Son et lumière* that triggers similar feelings as those expressed by Routhier at the beginning of the 20th century when he described his own "Québec at Night" – a visual performance that would have taken Routhier's breath away, had he been able to see it.

Somebody once called Québec a city dominated by shades of grey. For the past decade, however, the city has been alive with colour. No doubt, a sensitive mayor and a sensitized municipal service have had a great deal to do with this transformation. The proliferation of squares, gardens and fountains, the abundance of flowers, nighttime illuminations and festival streamers have all contributed to this visual renewal. During the holiday seasons, or at winter carnival time, Place Royale, the *rue du* Petit-Champlain, and the *côte de la* Fabrique become a kaleidoscope of Christmas decorations, exuberant shop windows and illuminated ice sculptures. Then fresh snow comes, turning the entire landscape into a fairy-tale village.

As the days and seasons succeed one another, light changes, explains Claudel Huot. "May, June, September and October are my favourite months. The tender green of spring inspires me most of all. It's a wondrous time of year. Ten days of visual symphony when light and vegetation create a soft and subtle palette."

In summer, the air thickens down by the river, rendered ever more unbearable by constant heat waves – not a time for touring and sight-seeing, but for intimate close-ups, for people watching in crowded places that confer a festive medieval mood on the city. The place is overrun with tourists – time for the photographer to take a vacation himself.

In winter, Québec explodes into light. It's the period of greatest contrast. The photographer can rush out after a storm to capture short-lived, at times surreal, images of purity. You have to be quick to take advantage of the ever-shifting contours shaped by the snow.

Québec plays with light all year round. Those living high above the river in Lévis understand this perfectly. For three centuries, artists have eloquently demonstrated that the place offers the best vantage point from which to view Champlain's city. Claudel Huot was himself a resident of Lévis, where he learned to study the movement of light as it spread over the storied city. A century after Adolphe-Basile Routhier, Huot's poetic images reveal exactly the same emotions.

Play of light on *rue* Claire-Fontaine near the Grand Theatre

Place Royale

Chiaroscuro

33

Rue Sainte-Anne, seen from Place d'Armes

Place d'Armes

The Seminary, Old Québec

THE LIGHTS OF QUÉBEC

The Old Port

City reflection

Ruelle du Magasin-du-Roi – Petit-Champlain neighbourhood

View from the courtyard

December magic at Place FAO

Snowy December

Rue du Petit-Champlain in the snow

December day, Place Royale

First snow, October, Place René-Lévesque

Blizzard, *rue du* Petit-Champlain

Dufferin Terrace in December,
and in the distance,
the Champlain Monument

The Chevalier House in the rain

Cap Diamant

Winter mist at the junction of *rues* Sainte-Ursule and Sainte-Geneviève

Between Two Shores

LIGHT PLAYS ON THE WATER

LIGHT PLAYS ON THE WATER

THE ST. LAWRENCE IS AN ADMIRABLE WORK OF NATURE, A MARVEL OF GRANDEUR AND OF BEAUTY. IN ITS ONWARD COURSE TO THE SEA, PASSING BY THE CITY OF CHAMPLAIN, IT TURNS TOWARDS THIS CHARMING SPOT, AS THOUGH IT WOULD LINGER TO CARESS IT STILL LONGER, AS THOUGH IT WOULD EXTEND ITS ARMS TO EMBRACE IT, SEEMING TO REGRET ITS SEPARATION; AND, IF THE TRAVELLERS WHO GLIDE OVER ITS SURFACE, COULD UNDERSTAND THE LANGUAGE OF THIS KING OF MIGHTY WATERS, THEY WOULD PROBABLY HEAR IT SAY: "BEHOLD, MY WELL BELOVED CITY, THE MOST BEAUTIFUL JEWEL OF MY CROWN!"

MARCHING ONWARD UNCEASINGLY, ITS WAVES PASS, SINK AND DISAPPEAR, BUT ARE REPLACED BY OTHERS WITH IMPEL THEM. THIS NOBLE RIVER IS THE ORNAMENT, THE CHARM, AND THE GREAT ATTRACTION OF THE PICTURESQUE CITY OF QUÉBEC.

ADOLPHE-BASILE ROUTHIER
Quebec at the Dawn of the 20th Century, 1900

Panorama seen from the Lévis Terrace

E VERY YEAR, SOMETHING MIRACULOUS HAPPENS TO THE WATERSCAPE THAT LIES before Québec. One fine morning in late autumn or early winter, they suddenly discover, with almost routine astonishment, that during the night the St. Lawrence River has started to freeze over, covering the surface with a skin of glittering ice crystals. Soon, the ice-breakers will be summoned to help winter navigation continue to operate without hindrance, for even the daily high tides cannot break the thickening crust. Until the turn of the 20th century, the riverside municipalities helped to maintain a route – an ice bridge, really – lined with fir trees that linked the two shores during the winter. When the spring thaw arrived, followed as it always was by the tumultuous break-up of the ice, a few reckless individuals defied the decision by the authorities to close the ice bridge, and sank into the frigid waters with all their gear.

The river changes constantly, day after day, month after month, from one season to the next. Grey or blue during the summer, the water's surface is sometimes tinged with shades of green, as if covered with a flaming substance to catch the setting sun as it slips contentedly beneath the horizon. On a clear evening, the river sports long streams of glowing colour emanating from a bridge of dazzling gold; beneath the cloud, it has the lyrical appearance of an abstract painting. In winter, the water sheds its shimmering colours and jettisons its continuity. Small floating islands dot the surface, surrounded in sunny weather by a myriad of blue pools. At slack water, between tides, the pools are like mirrors, reflecting the landscape formed by the two opposing headlands.

March light on the river

The effect is especially arresting at night, when the peaceful image of brightly lighted neighbourhoods is extended to infinity, as in a mirror seemingly splintered into thousands of tiny mosaics.

Almost forever, the historic capital has offered a handsome spectacle from the St. Lawrence River itself. In the 19th century, at a time when people came to Québec mainly by boat, several buildings were designed as a visual expression of the town from the river's perspective. In order to underline the prestige of the site and to impress the visitor, the rear façades of some buildings overlooking the waterfront were decorated with an enormous architectural *trompe-l'oeil*, such as the gable end of Laval University and the riverfront exterior of the old Post Office.

One evocative image of the St. Lawrence is the happy memory of a crossing between Québec and Lévis. What could be more invigorating that to observe, leaning over the rail of the prow at 20 below zero, the ship struggling to break the ice, or to confront a bracing northeaster in summer. Morning and night, the ferry's regulars

Homage to Ansel Adams: Morning light in September

One can never adequately describe the emotions stirred up by watching the ice break up and sensing the approach of spring in Québec. As the sun strikes the river's surface, the ice crumbles and breaks into pieces – small white islands that slowly drift apart in a sea of blue. At such a time, nothing beats standing on the bridge of the ferry, or stretching out on a bench in the Old Port, and relishing the penetrating warmth. As Mother Nature prepares for her rebirth, the warm air speeds up the spring thaw. With the Laurentians as a backdrop, the St. Lawrence assumes a new role in the landscape so beloved of residents and visitors alike. From the heights of the city, the spacious prospect stretches away, dominated by the isle of Orléans, the Pointe de Lévis cape and the Beauport hillsides.

The St. Lawrence originates deep inside the far reaches of the western continent, from the Great Lakes and the drainage systems of the northern territories. The river connects Québec to the seven seas. For four centuries its unconquered waters have welcomed fleets from around the world. Photographs dating from the second half the 19th century show the river swarming with sailing ships loading up their holds with pine and oak – natural resources to be used up for England's profit. By 1850, the six-month navigation period witnessed a stream of nearly a thousand vessels every year. An army of labourers and sailors invaded the Lower Town, creating a very special community. Lumber destined for export was loaded on rafts in the back country, then transported by raftsmen down the Ottawa river to Québec before being shipped out to English ports. As the population of Quebec was turned into a community of lumberjacks in the 19th century, the capital city itself became the key oceanic terminal for this vast colonial enterprise.

Today, however, the society that swarms the river's banks in summer has changed dramatically. And what a sight to behold, that of huge ocean-liners – veritable floating palaces – smoothly gliding into port just below Cap Diamant, radically altering the cityscape. The business district along the *rue du* Petit-Champlain – outdoor cafés, restaurants, museums and exhibition halls – once brimming with stevedores, is quite literally assaulted by affluent tourists from around the world. Québec, designated a World Heritage Site in 1985, now figures on the list of exotic destinations for the most prestigious shipping lines.

Every morning, the sunrise lights up Cap Diamant and the left bank; at dusk, Lévis surrenders itself to the rays of the setting sun, to the great delight of strollers who wander through the Old Port or along Dufferin Terrace. The St. Lawrence River will always play a key historical and artistic role in the life of the capital city, a front-row player in the tournament of light that, day or night, summer or winter, enlivens the majestic skyline of Champlain's city.

Spring flood on *rue* Dalhousie

A frosty morning on the Lévis shore

View inside the Bassin Louise

An early January morning, Dufferin Terrace

Late afternoon on the river

The Royal Battery in the early morning

At anchor

September light

October light on the river

Eel fisherman

The roofs of the Château and a boat on the river

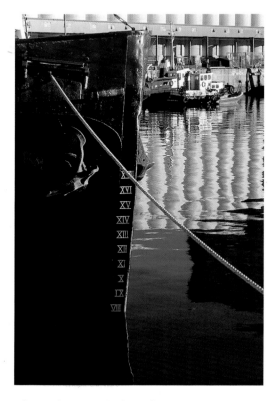

The Bassin Louise in the early morning

Peaceful moment

Lévis' lights shine on the river

Daybreak, October

Place Royale, the steeple of Notre-Dame-des-Victoires
with Lévis in the background

Québec under the weather!

Rowboats ploughing
the icy river

Nocturnal gleams,
December, Place Royale

Twilight in Place Royale

The Shapes and Textures of the Past

LIGHT FROM THE WALLS

The Shapes and Textures of the Past
LIGHT FROM THE WALLS

CONTEMPLATE THAT CHÂTEAU, THE ARCHITECTURE OF WHICH BELONGS TO THE MIDDLE AGES, BOLDLY PERCHED ON THE EDGE OF THE CRAGGED ROCK, ABOVE THE LOWER TOWN AND THE SUBURBS, AND SEE THE STAGGERING HEIGHT OF ITS TURRETS, TOWERS AND STEEPLES; THAT IS THE CHÂTEAU FRONTENAC.

NEARBY IS A GARDEN FULL OF HUGE TREES AND THROUGH THIS MASS OF FOLIAGE CAN BE SEEN AN OBELISK OF STONE.

FURTHER ON, BEHIND A CURTAIN OF GREAT ELM AND POPLAR TREES, LONG BUILDINGS CROWNED WITH CUPOLAS APPEAR; THESE ARE LAVAL UNIVERSITY AND THE QUÉBEC SEMINARY.

AND THERE, ON A LEVEL WITH THE RIVER, IS THE CUSTOMS HOUSE, WATCHING OVER THE PORT FROM THE HEIGHT OF ITS HARMONIOUS VAULTS AND BATHING IN THE WATERS ITS HANDSOME CORINTHIAN COLONNADE.

[…]

THE VIEW THEN BECOMES MORE EXTENSIVE, AND SOON DO YOU SEE THE LARGER BUILDINGS OF THE UPPER TOWN: THE TWO CATHEDRALS, ENGLISH AND FRENCH, WITH THEIR LOFTY STEEPLES, THE COURT HOUSE WITH ITS MAJESTIC PORTICO, THE CITY HALL, THE ROOF ONLY OF WHICH IS IN VIEW, AND THE PARLIAMENT BUILDING, WITH ITS HIGH TOWERS PROUDLY PROJECTING ON THE DISTANT HORIZON, IN THE MIDST OF A GROUP OF CHURCHES, THE STEEPLES OF WHICH ALONE ARE VISIBLE.

ADOLPHE-BASILE ROUTHIER
Quebec at the Dawn of the 20th Century, 1900

Chapel of the Québec Seminary

Walking along Québec's streets is like leafing through a history of world architecture, contained in the pages of an enormous book. There is a broad grammar of architectural styles – machicolations, pepperbox turrets, gun turrets and loopholes alternating with dormer windows, Ionic capitals, bow windows and mansard roofs – all evoking the tastes and habits of other eras.

Québec's cityscape embodies both its social values and the deep cultural currents that have fashioned its people at different times. Houses, religious buildings, institutions and military establishments all bear living witness to the close connections the Québécois have had with France, England and the United States – a close neighbour that has played an active role in the cultural history of the St. Lawrence River Valley. And all this historic evidence reveals a social crossbreeding that has helped to define a common identity unique in the world.

In the Basse-Ville – or Lower Town – the area around Place Royale, hard by the St. Lawrence, has the appeal and appearance of a small 18th-century French provincial town. The semi-detached, two- or three-storey stone houses, capped with steeply sloping roofs, at times give the stroller the illusion of wandering down a historic street in old Rouen, La Rochelle, or some other town in northeastern France, whence the first occupants of this part of Champlain's city had set forth. The same feelings, still more intimate, strike anyone roaming the Latin Quarter, along the old walls in the Upper Town (Haute-Ville).

Church tower

The French contribution to the fabric of the place is also demonstrated by the classical architecture of the old religious institutions, notably Québec's Basilica, designed by Gaspard Chaussegros de Léry (1682-1756). Despite the frequent fires that plague this wintry corner of the world, part of the Québec Seminary – training ground for the lay and clerical élites – as well as some sections of the Ursuline convent and that of the Hôtel-Dieu Augustinian nursing sisters still stand as testimony to French provincial architecture during the time of the "Sun King."

This French presence is bound up not only with the style, but also the methods, of construction, as well as the myriad details concerning the structural, utilitarian and esthetic components. Should you find yourself standing beside the bust of Louis XIV in Place Royale, you can, simply by a quick glance overhead, identify the various roofing methods used at the time of New France: cedar shingles, lapped planks, cover-joint planks, slate, metal sheeting – flat or corrugated. The old municipal regulations favoured non-flammable materials, and from the beginning of the 17th century, the early provincial administrators – the *Intendants* – laid down a whole series of laws compelling the use of stone construction and to meticulously respect – under threat of a fine or even demolition – the exclusive use of stone right down to the door frames. That was how Québec grew to become a city of rock and stone, a walled town of such special character.

England, in its turn, has left an imprint on the cityscape. The largest part of Québec *intra muros* – within the walls – belongs to this second cultural movement. Rough cast rustic walls give way to smooth, plain-cut stone; sharply angled roofs now stand side by side with gentler slopes; double-shuttered windows alternate with leaded bay windows and large-paned sash windows. Everywhere there are portals in the Doric, Ionic or Corinthian orders – juxtapositions and symmetry that are the city's architectural hallmark. It's in the urban warp and woof of the cape that Albion's contribution can be appreciated at its proper worth. The streets with names like Buade,

"Architexture"

The Seminary in the early morning

Saint-Denis, Saint-Louis, and Sainte-Ursule introduce rows of houses of great elegance and decorum. A striking-looking Anglican cathedral towering over its Roman Catholic neighbour – architecture remains a symbol of power – was inspired by the church of St. Martin's-in-the-Fields in London. Several institutions, including the old prison that has been turned into a school, the Customs House and army buildings, are in keeping with this impetus which was brought to a halt by fire and demolition.

The Parliament Building, the city hall, the former courthouse, the old prison located on the Plains of Abraham, the city gates, a number of chapels and churches, the old fire-stations, the Château Frontenac, the Capitol Theatre, the Palais railway station, and various streets yield an architectural showcase, a breathtaking eclecticism boldly mixing together French, British and American styles in works, if not always harmonious, at least highly fantastical. The capital's eclectic quality thus synthesizes the main influences that have moulded the city and the land, and in the process conveys a way of uniting the neo-Gothic, the neo-Renaissance and the neo-medieval with a contemporary period of renewal as an urban centre that gets ready to celebrate its third centenary.

In spite of its ever-present past, Québec is also a modern city. If the 20th century brings with it the pediment, the column, the entablature in the classic Beaux-Arts manner, there are a great many buildings that display the functional and esthetic simplicity of Art Deco and other international styles that were in vogue between the two world wars. The Palais Montcalm, Price House – Québec's first skyscraper-inspired by the urban designs of our neighbours to the south, and a number of cube-shaped, flat-roofed buildings are witness to this modern impulse.

Québec therefore takes on the appearance of a city filled with architectural contrasts where French classicism and British neoclassicism blend in with the neo-Gothic and neo-Renaissance. It is a sort of western-world eclecticism brought over by the France of Napoleon III, the England of Queen Victoria, and the United States. These styles join together with the simple lines of the 20th century to form, over the years, a unique architectural tapestry, where shapes, materials, colours, textures and décor confirm an exceptional character, a diversity that never ceases to astonish the watchful and sensitive passerby.

Curve

Light on the wall

Home improvements

Shadows over Place Royale

Quiet morning, at the corner of *rues* Laval and Hébert

Architectural perspective – Walls of history

Théâtre du Conservatoire, at the corner of *rues* Elgin and Saint-Stanislas

Remnants of the bankers' district, *rue* Saint-Pierre

Rue Saint-Jean

Dusk, the "blue hour", *rue* d'Auteuil

Ancestral houses, corner of Sainte-Famille and Hébert

Rue Dalhousie

Daybreak, *rue* Dalhousie

Diptych

Light on the walls, *rue* Mont-Carmel

First snow, *rue* Christie in the heart of the Latin Quarter

Rue Notre-Dame, Place Royale

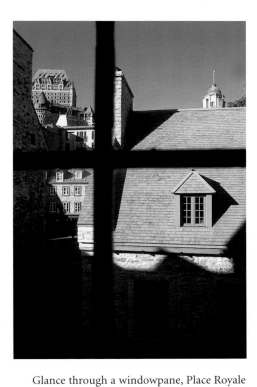

Glance through a windowpane, Place Royale

Winter texture

December morning at the junction of *rues* Saint-Jean,
Couillard, Garneau and *côte de la* Fabrique

A fine address, *rue du* Petit-Champlain

Rue du Cul-de-Sac

Winter's arrived

A fine address, *rue du* Petit-Champlain

Rue du Cul-de-Sac

Winter's arrived

Fairyland on Parliament Hill

Customs House, Old Port

Morning Light, *rue* Couillard

Rue Couillard after the rain

Gardens and the Colours of Québec

NATURE IN THE CITY

Gardens and the Colours of Québec
NATURE IN THE CITY

See, there is a suspended garden where urchins are yelling at play. It is on a slope and looks as though it would tumble down the hill. But no, its foundation is so solid that it serves as a support for a second suspended garden. The tourist continues his uphill walk, but stops again and wonders what to do next. Will he take a rest among the flowers and trees of the garden, will he go on following the steep round of many windings as though it were an enormous spiral? Or will he climb that other iron staircase on his left, in order to get sooner to his journey's end?

[…]

More steps to mount will bring him in view of another garden in rear of the Château Frontenac; and finally another staircase, the last but not the least, as it has upwards of a hundred steps, will bear him to the crest of the glacis, above which still stands the Citadel. That is where he will be rewarded for the pains he has taken, and we can readily predict that he will forget all fatigue and stand enraptured, finding but these words to express his delight: "Oh! How beautiful! Oh! How beautiful!"

Adolphe-Basile Routhier
Quebec at the Dawn of the 20th Century, 1900

The Plains of Abraham

ACITY'S SOUL DEPENDS TO A LARGE EXTENT ON ITS RELATIONSHIP WITH NATURE — the contrasts between wood and stone as well as the harmony between architecture and green spaces. Nothing could be more pleasant than a stroll across a landscaped square, columned with large trees, that eventually leads the way to parks, gardens and unobtrusive oases that suddenly loom up through, say, the iron grills of private properties or around the corner of a small lane, in some private courtyard. In cities like Boston, London, Stockholm, or in Old Philadelphia, the visitor is often awestruck by a lush urban gardenscape. Québec figures among ecology-friendly cities. The purity of its air and waters makes for crystal-clear views of the city's coutours in every season of the year, and is responsible for its dense and lush vegetation, which in summer, stands out in sharp contrast with rock and stone.

Traditionally, the religious communities maintained huge gardens to embellish their places of meditation, provide flowers for the altars of their nearby chapel and the cathedral, and also to grow medicinal plants, seasoning herbs, fruit and vegetables. The old blueprints of church buildings, and those of a number of civic structures, always include precise designs for the inclusion of gardens on the property. Some of the old treatises sometimes carry interesting details concerning the horticultural techniques in urban gardens. The governor's residence, the Intendant's mansion, the Ursuline convent and that of the Hôtel-Dieu were all endowed with such enclosures governed by strict and geometrically arranged patterns, in the French style.

Saint-Louis Gate

A quiet gossip, Montmorency Park

As ever, the spirit of the French garden hovers over the monument to Joan of Arc, on the edge of the Plains of Abraham. There, a harmonious symphony of some 50 annual flower species and a hundred more varieties of perennials plays out every summer. At dusk, a kind of magic suffuses the air, conferring a surreal feeling on the place. Nearby, the recent landscape design on Parliament Hill follows in the same style of classical axes. For a French neo-Renaissance monument, it's only fitting than the gardens surrounding it breathe the same spirit.

Flying over Québec or looking down on the city from the surrounding heights, one realizes that the capital is an enormous garden, despite the imposing presence of stone. In every direction, huge trees fill the gaps between buildings, rustling and obscuring the latter. In his *Regard infini* [Infinite Gaze], the poet Pierre Morency associates Québec's green spaces – parks, squares and public gardens – with its history, from architecture right down to the words engraved on the bronze statues, striking haughty poses here and there in the city. In spring time, the poet intimates, enclosed in soft green and haloed by the delicate lilac blossoms and apple blossoms, the figures in this bronze gallery seem to confide countless centuries-old secrets to the saunterers in a sort of interaction that lasts until autumn, ending amid an explosion of blazing colour.

To everything however, there is a season. When the time comes, crocuses, tulips and daffodils that emerge from the ground in spring, must give way to the summer's lush carpet of brightly coloured perennials and annuals, which in turn are supplanted by the fireworks of autumn's foliage. It is difficult not to succumb to the misty image of these parks, gardens, groves and trees as they gradually recede behind veils of rain in October and November. Then snow and hoarfrost come, clinging to everything and turning it all into a huge black and white tableau.

The rich texture of Québec's flora is also revealed by tree-lined thoroughfares like Grande-Allée – which, until the end of the 19th century, was regarded as the city's own Champs-Élysées – as well as in the many wooded parks dotted with inviting benches, and by the conspicuous maples, elms and linden trees that enhance the approaches to several houses and office buildings. The flora literally burst forth on the Citadel's open periphery, in the broad expanse of the Champs-de-Bataille and in the enclosed woodland formed by the flanks of the escarpment that stretches beyond the city limits. Thus the edge of the cape offers wanderers a stunning natural environment brought to life by the constantly changing topography – an enchanted setting that evokes the various stages of the country's history.

The Plains of Abraham are the heart and soul of Québec, and a grassy rendez-vous for innumerable get-togethers and festivities. In 1908, they were turned into a vast open-air theatre where the entire population participated in the reenactment, costumes and all, of the age of Champlain. On Saint-Jean-Baptiste Day, Quebec's national holiday, the city's plateaus and hillsides are home to enormous bonfires – a centuries-old tradition. Its hiking and cross-country ski trails provide excursions through a breathless panorama where the land embraces the sea. The same sense of communion with the natural world and the river enlivens picnics with friends or family in the refreshing shade of the tall trees, while the youngsters enthusiastically climb over the old cannons that haven't fired a shot for ages and have now become a scenic background for souvenir photographs.

In winter, nothing is more exciting than the view of Cap Diamant from the hills of Lévis. Seen through the mists rising from the ice-covered river, the escarpment looks like a lyrical, abstract painting. In fact, one loses count of the number of artists, both local and coming from elsewhere, who have rendered with masterful skill and unusual sensitivity the spectacular natural setting that is the city of Champlain.

Nature's contradiction

First snow, *rue* d'Auteuil

First snow, *rue* d'Auteuil

The month of May, *rue* d'Auteuil

Côte de la Fabrique

The Plains of Abraham, May

The Plains of Abraham, February

Winter, Maizerets estate

Portal of the Anglican bishop's palace

In the shade of the oak trees, *rue des* Jardins

NATURE IN THE CITY

Pond, Maizerets estate

Water lilies on the Maizerets estate

Autumn Fantasy

View from the garden, *rue* Laval

Sir George-Étienne Cartier, witness to the seasons

Montmorency Park: Frost on the apple trees

The painter Francesco Iacurto in Montmorency Park

Montmorency Park

Cloistered wall, *rue* Hamel

The old black walnut tree, *rue* Sainte-Anne

Light in May

NATURE IN THE CITY

Place d'Armes

Place d'Armes

Panoramas and Perspectives

THE URBAN LANDSCAPE

Panoramas and Perspectives
THE URBAN LANDSCAPE

As we scale its heights, the horizon grows under our eyes, and offers to us at each step, new objects for our admiration. At every turn, we discover new beauties. Perspective succeeds perspective in a train of dazzling and majestic gradations; and contemplating the grandeur of the spectacle, together with the variety of its aspects, we are at a loss which to admire most.

The superb chain of the Laurentians away in the North, the graceful isle of Orléans, with its wood-clad hills on the East, the high promontories of Lévis on the South, and finally the rock of Québec, at the base of which the great St. Lawrence, with its tributary the St. Charles, murmur and sparkle — all form a majestic panorama, whose giant-like proportions stand out silhouetted against the sky.

Certainly, this coliseum of nature is a magnificent work, and the man who laid there the foundations of a city, had within him a love for the grand and the beautiful.

Adolphe-Basile Routhier
Quebec at the Dawn of the 20th Century

Church towers in Old Québec

Q UÉBEC OFFERS A FULL RANGE OF LANDSCAPES. ITS PROMONTORY PROVIDES AN outlook for a constantly changing view, just as the Pointe de Lévis cape, right across the river, is itself an out-standing vantage point, both spatial and temporal. The natural characteristics of the place, complete with an ever-changing topography, make it pure heaven to stroll through the town. It's a place where stunning natural and urban vistas simultaneously vie for one's attention. Whichever way he turns, the stroller is sure to enjoy thrilling views – narrow or wide-angled.

The views of Québec have a make-believe quality. Those most often depicted by writers and artists are the ones observed from the Lévis hilltops, but the city as viewed from the water is just as breathtaking. Hundreds of thou-sands of visitors understand this, and have taken the ferry connecting the two shorelines in order to sketch their own postcards of, say, Cap Diamant or the Château Frontenac. Once on the other side, the more curious among them – and the camera fiends – will scale the heights, or climb the red stairway to take a memorable stroll through Lévis' old town. Feelings become most intense when you reach the terrace, opposite its counterpart on the Québec side, christened Dufferin in honour of the famous 19th-century British governor-general. In 1900, Adolphe-Basile Routhier marvelled at the view of Québec from the hillside of Lévis:

View from the Seminary tower

Rue Saint-Denis

"Lévis is one of Québec's beauties, as Québec is Lévis's greatest charm. I mean that we *Québécois* regard Lévis as one of the most picturesque sights upon which we may gaze, and that *Lévisiens* have the advantage of seeing Québec better than we do ourselves. They are quite at liberty to nurse the fond belief that it is to please them and for their benefit that the city of Champlain increases, and that the number of spires, cupolas and domes is always becoming greater. They may also harbour the illusion that Québec is every night illuminated for their personal gratification, and that the myriads of stars which they see shining in the deep azure of the northern skies are there to dazzle and charm them."

For Routhier, this panorama was not a one-way visual exercise: "They return the compliment, however the great variety of its colourings prevent us from any wearisome feeling when viewing the magnificent panorama which Lévis presents. Those colourings vary with every hour of the day, now they are bright and then they become shady and veiled, the morning sees them bathed in transparent mist and at night they are ablaze with the rays of the setting sun."

The magic moment for these panoramas occurs at dawn and at twilight: "Morning is the time when Lévisiens may view Québec in all its southern splendour. But for us Québécois, the hour of sunset is that in which Lévis can be seen clothed in her richest garb; it is then flooded with radiance and rays of ruby-coloured light shine upon her spires."

Added to the area's natural beauty – the river, the isle of Orléans, the Beauport hillsides and the basin connecting the historic capital to the seven seas – are a host of landlocked, less extensive, scenes: squares, parks, gardens, and entire streets sometimes attractively overlooking the water. These picturesque townscapes – a happy union between architecture and nature – are reminiscent of the great cultures of France, Great Britain and the United States, that have forged the soul of the capital city. The old stones, the pointed roofs, the large chimneys, the arrow-like steeples, the crosses and the eclectic turrets, evoke, each in its own way, a piece of the land's history. The landscapes of 18th-century France, in and around Place Royale, display a very different face to those of the 19th-century, near the slopes of the Citadel or in the streets that run alongside the Ramparts erected at the time of the British garrison. In the same way, the intimate link between the Lower Town and the river banks, palpable down to the smell of the sea and the cry of the gulls, has nothing in common other than the presence of the water, with the relation of the Upper Town to the river: in the blustery air and wind squalls, the view from Dufferin Terrace and the Ramparts seems lofty and reassuring.

But Québec is about much more than all this. It is also about the serendipitous discoveries that one makes simply by raising or lowering one's head, or when mindlessly looking left or right, discoveries that nonetheless connect the stroller to a powerful symbolic element of the historic site. This is a city of monuments, of church steeples, of towers and official buildings, each displaying styles linked intimately to a specific school or a precise epoch. This stylistic variety, which confers a personal touch on the urban centre and makes it stand out from all others, remains one of the keys to the city's incomparable charm.

The lure of a panorama, of a closed site or an accidental view – as only the historic capital offers so generously – stems first of all from its richness as a symbol, as regards history, art and culture. Nature itself, that timeless major component of the urban landscape, reinforces and heightens the historic and symbolic contents. All those qualities are everywhere present in the landscape of Québec, to the delight of its residents and the thousands of visitors who each year are nourished by its unique allure and constant evolution.

Bassin Louise, grey shadows in March

First snow, December, Bassin Louise

December wonderland

Rue du Petit-Champlain

General store, Place Royale

A snowy dawn, *rue du* Petit-Champlain

Feast of light, *rue* Dalhousie

Night scene in Place Royale

View from the Ramparts

Rue Saint-Denis

Riverside view of Place Royale

The Latin Quarter

Place Royale seen from Montmorency Park

An urban frescoe

Old Québec seen from Pointe à Carcy in the port

Daybreak, summer solstice

Time to set sail

Hibernation (Bassin Louise)

Petit-Champlain neighbourhood

Daybreak on *rue du* Petit-Champlain

Rue du Cul-de-Sac

Escalier Casse-Cou (Breakneck Steps)

Of Flesh and Bronze
IN THE FOOTPRINTS OF HISTORY

Of Flesh and Bronze
IN THE FOOTPRINTS OF HISTORY

Even before he draws his last breath, man loses his power of speech. Yet his thoughts and works survive him; and that is one of the main features which makes him bear a certain resemblance to his Creator. What a number of illustrious men, who have been dead for centuries, still speak to us in that way! When their works become a mass of ruins, the remaining stones talk in their stead. Doubtless they are not all eloquent. There are cities in which the stones have no language of their own. But Québec is one of those spots in which the memory of the past is awakened at every step, and where all things seem to raise their voices in proclaiming those who are no more. [...]

Should tourists wish to find out what famous discoverer first took possession of that wild land, in the name of Christian civilization; of that historic spot upon which now stands our city, they have but to descend to the shores of the St. Charles river, at the confluence of the Lairet stream. They will there find a humble monument, which will relate the tale, carved upon a block of Laurentian granite. That is the spot upon which, nearly four centuries ago, a sailor from Brittany first planted the flag of France.

Adolphe-Basile Routhier
Quebec at the Dawn of the 20th Century

The Anglican Cathedral – Holy Trinity

IN ROME, THE ETERNAL CITY, EVERY TIME THAT MUNICIPAL WORKERS STICK THEIR shovels in the ground, they come across some vestige of the past whose discovery brings their work to an abrupt halt. The promoters of a new construction project are occasionally obliged to suspend the work while they await the verdict of the archaeologists. Getting a permit to resume their activities is far from certain in such a situation.

The cities that make up the crown jewels of UNESCO's World Heritage list, such as Rome and Québec, offer up priceless historical treasures that are protected – at least in principle. The evidence of a distant past leaves its mark not just in archival documents and museum pieces, but also on the urban network – that is, the architectural make-up and various memorials, those glorious chapters in a great book cast, as it were, in bronze.

That Québec is a city of special historic importance is a given. The site chosen by Samuel de Champlain in 1608 was retained for its strategic value. From the outset, the *Abitation* was designed as a fort. A little later, a royal battery took up its position in the river to discourage any ships from attempting to penetrate inland. The cliffs acted as a bastion, then an unobtrusive but powerful citadel arose to give the cape a new profile. After the victorious siege of 1759, an event that altered the face of America, the English quickly set about improving these defences. To pass through the city's gates is to relive important events in the country's history.

Place Royale, 1759

With a little imagination, simply roaming the streets of Québec will transport you back in time, say, into the distant echo of religious ceremonies unfolding in the cathedrals – Catholic or the more imposing Anglican – and of matins in the convents of the Augustinian Sisters and the Ursulines. Both groups had arrived in 1639, the first to take care of the sick, the orphans, and the underprivileged, and the second to take charge of the education of young women. At times you almost believe that you can hear the sound of state funerals, processions, or celebrations in honour of the saints of the Gregorian Calendar, the forty-hours' adoration … In fact, countless missionaries had set forth from this ecclesiastical headquarters, whose glorious mandate it was to convert the "Savages," as the native peoples were known at the time of the Jesuit pioneers and Monseigneur de Laval. Québec – a focal point for history and religion – is a sacred acropolis where arrows and crosses capped by a crowing rooster peer forth in every direction, signalling the awakening and dissemination of the Catholic faith. Today

Sweet memories, *rue* Couillard –
the Seventies

The walls have a story to tell

Quiet! Action! – *rue* Couillard

the founders of the old institutions and the grandees of the Church are glorified in the form of bronze statues, in the middle of a square or in commemorative relief in some quiet corner of a religious community garden.

Québec's sense of history reveals itself in all its fullness on Parliament Hill. The façade of the Parliament Building stands out as if it were a huge history book, sheltering in its recesses, as at the Louvre, the great figures who have shaped the country. The gardens are peopled with those giants who, since the turn of the 20th century, played a major role in Québec's evolution towards modernity: from Honoré Mercier, the most celebrated political figure of the 19th century, to René Lévesque, that splendid head of state who was so close to his own people, and in between, Adélard Godbout and Jean Lesage, two colourful premiers.

Again with a little help from the imagination, walking down *rues* Saint-Jean and Saint-Louis, one can follow in the footsteps of the early 17th- and 18th-century explorers as they went to the Governor's mansion or the palace of the Intendant of New France to receive their marching orders: to build a fort on the shores of the Great Lakes, or set up trading posts in the American midwest, along the Mississippi and its tributaries. Other celebrated figures, like Iberville, set out for Hudson Bay in order to wage war against the English. So many living legends and

heroes came to kneel and pray in the basilica or the Church of Notre-Dame-des-Victoires and there receive the blessing of their church.

History is everywhere in Québec. Great figures and episodes from our past live and breathe in the old libraries of the capital and in the archival treasures of the 300-year-old religious institutions. There you can find ancient treatises on surgery and pharmacy, even manuals on exorcism dating from medieval France. The museums overflow with works and artefacts that bring back times gone by, and a number of exhibition halls specialize in reconstructing the historic battles waged in Québec. The fortification walls, the various architectural styles, the narrow streets, all lead us down history's path. The city's toponomy recalls the names of the great figures of old, of commerce and trade, or the brilliant feats commemorated in the names given to the squares and thoroughfares: Talon, Frontenac, Bourlamarque, Bougainville… Governors, Intendants, soldiers, and, extraordinarily, even the men of General Wolfe's army who bombarded and destroyed Québec in 1759, all are given a place of honour. In a society whose motto is *Je me souviens* (I remember), one must not forget to salute the bronze statue of its first historian, François-Xavier Garneau. A line of famous photographers – the Livernois family – have for 120 years, from 1859-1974, preserved for posterity all the famous men and women of the capital and continue to skilfully follow the progress of Champlain's city in our own time.

History is equally present in the hearts and collective memories of ordinary people. This interest in the past is manifest in the many lively publications and periodicals, in the activities of historical and heritage societies, and in the unique cultural character of the city where the confluence of styles and customs begets its gastronomy, the visual arts, theatre and other performance arts. At the start of a new millennium, Québec looks forward confidently as a city with a rich past and a bright future.

Taking Flight, the monument dedicated to the Christian Brothers

Joan of Arc

The Musée de la civilisation

Champlain, founder of Québec in 1608

Monument in memory of Honoré Mercier

Rue du Trésor and *rue* Buade

Sound the festive trumpet! Detail: Champlain statue

Saint-Louis Gate, on a luminous summer night (pp. 202-203)

Statue of Monseigneur de Laval

The Musée de la civilisation and the Québec Seminary

Parliament Hill

Notre Dame Basilica in December

Sunday Mass at Notre Dame Basilica

Seminary chapel and the Musée
de l'Amérique française

Saint-Jean Gate on
a luminous winter night
(pp. 210-211)

208

Those who shaped history …

Silhouettes on the Ramparts

Rue des Jardins, Donnacona and des Ursulines

Interior courtyard of the Québec Seminary, photographed on a September morning

Statue of François-Xavier Garneau

The old prison, today part of the Musée du Québec

The Rites of Summer and Winter

FESTIVE CITY

The Rites of Summer and Winter
FESTIVE CITY

As may be inferred, Québec is not a dead city and has a fair share of amusements. One undeniable fact is that Québec is the place where children amuse themselves. It seems to me that it is a regular paradise for children. In the very centre of the city there are the Esplanade, the Terrace and the Glacis, which they may use as perfectly safe playgrounds and in winter they have the best natural slides in the world, almost at their very doors; the skating rinks are open during the day and in the evening. [...]

In summer, amusements change, of which there are still any number: ball games of all kinds, cricket and golf are very popular. [...] Summer is also the fishing and boating season, and may be called the "American Season," for our neighbours from the United States invade the town, and Québec becomes their summer resort, this fact is all the more evident as most of the Québécois are away.

Adolphe-Basile Routhier
Quebec at the Dawn of the 20th Century, 1900

Interior courtyard, the Ursuline convent

ANTHROPOLOGISTS HAVE ALWAYS TAKEN A KEEN INTEREST IN THE CELEBRATIONS AND rituals that are a feature of societies around the world. Their observations and analyses have led them to establish a single fact that is generally true for every situation: a celebration, they believe, calls for three basic components.

The first summons up the past. In order to put themselves in a celebratory mood, men and women from every culture are encouraged to step back in time and rediscover their roots. On Quebec's national holiday, for example, as the crowds thronging the sidewalks look on, the past is borne along in a procession of allegorical floats that represent some glorious episodes from their history – the customs and costumes that recall their origins, the ancient and modern exploits that help define a society and stimulate its pride. Just as you celebrate the birthday of a loved one, you think about the year that's coming to a close, and evoke happy memories as you recount an old anecdote or leaf through a photo album in order to revive the events that have stood out in that particular time frame, and cement the ties as confirmed at such a moment. Without this ability to recover time past, there would be no celebration in the first place.

Once the past has been "recovered," one can give joy full rein, letting it burst forth unrestrained. Celebration then moves into full gear, assisted by a panoply of symbols and accessories, and achieves a kind of ecstasy: lights and

Party time at Place Royale

Easter vigil in the church of Notre-Dame de Québec

multicoloured ornaments, costumes, champagne, feasts, games and the ubiquitous party masks, sweeping away all inhibitions and taboos.

The third stage of the celebration occurs after the exultations have subsided, and constitutes what anthropologists sum up as "hopeful vision for the future" – in other words, the very reason for celebrating. In order to be free of one's impulses and anxieties, to take stock and properly plan for the future, one needs to slow down from time to time to catch one's breath and restore one's sense of identity. The cycle of festivals that marks the rhythm of the year and punctuates the life of each individual underlines this basic need. Time then to talk hopefully of nation-building, of the sense of pride reawakened by recalling heroes past and present, of bright days ahead, of encouragement and optimism that one feels as life goes on. Celebrating, therefore, seems to be a necessity; in fact, it is an obligation.

In 1900, Sir Adolphe-Basile Routhier published his fine book, *Quebec at the Dawn of the 20th Century*, to celebrate the capital of North America's French-speaking people and its entry into the new century. The book itself is arranged like a veritable festival, marking not only the changing of a century, but also the forthcoming commemoration, in 1908, of Québec's founding by Samuel de Champlain, three centuries earlier.

Routhier begins by retracing the history of the city and the surrounding region in lively detail. All the illustrious figures and great deeds of Québec's collective journey are recreated in the reader's mind. The festival takes on a brilliant life of its own in the author's impressive word pictures, aided by the sumptuously produced volume itself, bound in leather with gilt edges, and enhanced by pen-and-ink drawings and photographs. In its jewel-box setting, Québec explodes in word and image. A whole chapter – "Québec in the 20th Century" – is devoted to a forecast of the city's development, to a dream of the historic capital's future direction. Reading about these "hopeful visions for the future" shows just how farsighted the author was!

A century on, the selection of Claudel Huot's splendid photographs evokes the same sense of celebration. Like Routhier's, our project is a celebration in every sense of the word. Today, in 2001, technology gives us the means to show what's happening rather than just writing about it. It's not that words have become obsolete, but the creative image can subtly convey the emotions aroused by the appeal of a historic city, often in sensitive and poetic terms.

Québec is a festive space. Its skyline, natural beauty and charm all give rise to feelings of conviviality and nostalgia, the countless pleasures of life and cyclical eruptions of joy. For the Québécois, as well as all the francophones of America, the city of Champlain remains not only a gem of a place to cherish, protect and show off to advantage, but also a reassuring pledge of continuity.

Without doubt it is this richness that explains the ease and happiness with which its citizens invariably embrace the art of celebrating, whether it's a slice of history reenacted on stage, during an enchanting festival, or at winter carnival time. The whole city and the combined creative talents of its people lend a hand to keep Old Québec alive, through traditional and modern rites, opening it up to the world at large.

Pagan festival at Place Taschereau

Interior courtyard, the Québec Seminary

Saint-Louis Gate

Romantic ride on *rue* Sainte-Anne

Daybreak, Royal Battery

Skating rink in Place d'Youville seen through a slit in Saint-Jean Gate

Place Royale, *rue* Dalhousie

Party Time!

Make believe!

Bois-de-Coulonge Park

Le Vendôme, *côte de la* Montagne (Mountain Hill)

Celebrating on Parliament Hill

Rue Saint-Jean in holiday mood

Reenactment of an ancient market day at Place Royale,
seen here in the shadow of the church of Notre-Dames-des-Victoires

Let the festival begin!

Two châteaux

Rue Saint-Louis

Rue du Cul-de-Sac, behind the Chevalier House

Looking down on the Petit-Champlain neighbourhood from the top of *l'escalier* Casse-Cou (Breakneck Steps)

Stair landings,
l'escalier Casse-Cou
(Breakneck Steps)

Calèches in the Governor's Garden with Lévis in the distance

Fallen angel

QUÉBEC, CITY OF THE SENSES

Bust of Sir Winston Churchill, at the foot
of Saint-Louis Gate, *rue* Saint-Louis

QUÉBEC IS A CITY MADE FOR THE ARTIST. IN THIS REGARD, IT IS WITHOUT COMPARISON anywhere in the world. For three centuries, painters, engravers, and photographers by the hundreds have left behind a richly generous record of the city's imperishable charms. Not a single man of letters, or scholar, has glimpsed its promontory or penetrated its walled city without attempting to express the powerful emotions that he feels, without marvelling at the irresistible spell cast by this city blessed by the gods.

Québec's remarkable reputation rests, above all, on the intense northern light that reshapes the landscape as the hours and seasons succeed one another, from the soft greens of May, to the sustained blue of fine September days, and the rosy pinks and astonishing purple tones of winter dusks. Dawns, in the ever-changing panoramas, are limpid and pure as the very air. And, every evening in fair weather, the day subsides beneath a golden bridge that sets the river afire in a blaze of orange and blue, stretching towards infinity. The night brings its own unforgettable spectacle, especially during the winter, around Place Royale and *rue du* Petit-Champlain, when snow flurries redefine the layout of the streets, flooded with multi-coloured light, muffling sound and soothing the soul. As an alert chronicler of the changing weather, Claudel Huot knows how to respond quickly to such visual stimuli.

Québec is a maritime city, too, a place that for centuries has never failed to excite those who can appreciate the unique worth of age-old places, rich in the adventure and promise of its sea-going destiny.

Above all, Québec is a city soaked in history. Its site has always been coveted for its strategic value, and the three great powers – France, England and the United States – vied for control, each nation leaving its seal on the territory. Even today, and especially in its architecture and lifestyle, the city bears living witness to this network of historic influences, its inhabitants the heirs to an outward-looking society. As long ago as the 18th century, the great explorers struck out from the city's fortified walls to begin taming the rest of the North American continent. Later, armies of missionaries forsook the city to bring the "good news" – of Catholicism and French culture – to the four corners of the globe, with no colonizing aspirations.

Québec is a city of landscapes, a huge and continually embellished garden, a place of festival and celebration that each year welcomes millions of visitors who come to share an original way of life. Summer and winter, they flock to the city, anticipating the warm hospitality for which Québec and its people are justly renowned.

Ultimately, Québec is a city of the senses, and a powerful symbol. For Québécois as a whole, it remains a unique national capital, the seat of government where, since 1791, its elected officials have administered the rules and regulations of the first parliamentary democracy in the Americas. It is also the centre of the main political and cultural institutions that are the foundation of its status as a modern state. For America's francophones, Québec represent a welcoming and generous source, a wellspring that enshrines and promotes the values maintained by a thousand lineages formed by some 15 generations of children spread throughout Canada and the United States. Like no other city, Québec is the symbol of a nation's birth.

All things considered, Québec is the sum total of its people, yesterday and today. Step by step, in his individual way, Claudel Huot follows in that bright heritage.

SELECT BIBLIOGRAPHY

BEAUDET, Louis. "Québec, ses monuments anciens et modernes ... ou Vademecum des citoyens et des touristes," (1890), *Cahiers d'histoire,* No. 25, Québec, Société historique de Québec, 198 pp.
The manuscript of this tourist guide – the most complete and fully documented on 19th -century Québec – was gathering dust in the archives of the Québec Seminary until the city's historic society decided to publish it in 1890. It was written by a Seminary priest, and constitutes an impressive record of the historic city.

CHAMPLAIN, Samuel de. *The works of Samuel de Champlain,* edited by Henry P. Biggar, 6 volumes, Toronto, The Champlain Society, 1922-1936.
The writings of the founder of the City of Québec are an indispensable research tool for understanding the nascent intellectual, religious and political contexts of Canada's ancient capital. There are various editions, complete with plates, available for more inquiring readers.

CHARBONNEAU, André, DESLOGES, Yvon and LAFRANCE, Marc. *Québec, The Fortified City: From the 17th to the 19th Century,* Parks Canada, Canadian Government Publishing Centre, Supply and Services Canada, 1982, 491 pp.
A team of Parks Canada historians describe the political and military circumstances, construction techniques and urban development of Québec under both the French and English regimes, including Lord Dufferin's efforts to preserve the antiquated fortifications.

DE VOLPI, Charles P. *Québec: A Pictorial Record. Historical Prints and Illustrations of the City of Québec, Province of Québec, Canada, 1608-1875.* Toronto, Longman Canada Limited, 1971, 190 pp.
A book containing 186 plates of Québec City, selected from early engravings on the capital. Each drawing is accompanied by a brief description and analysis. A good synthesis of the iconography of the historic city.

DORION, Henri, dir., et BLANCHET, Johanne, coll. *Cités souvenir, cités d'avenir. Villes du patrimoine mondial,* Québec, Musée de la civilisation, 1991, 195 pp.
A description of the 20 cities then recognized by UNESCO as World Heritage Sites. Historian Michel Lessard writes about Québec, one of the World Heritage Sites, and explains how it became a member of this exclusive club.

DOUGHTY, Arthur George. *Quebec under two flags, a brief history of the city of Quebec.* Québec, The Quebec News Co., 1903, 424 pp.
A history of the city of Québec, the battleground and capital of an empire.

DUVAL, André. *Québec romantique,* Montréal, Boréal Express, 1978, 285 pp.

The author of this sensitive study of 19th-century Québec bases his thesis on the eyewitness reports of travellers and writers. "The book's originality stems from the richly varied opinions about a city that everyone knows by reputation and many have had the curiosity and the opportunity to visit." A volume to help you fall in love with Québec.

HARE, John, LAFRANCE, Marc and RUDDELL, David-Thierry. *Histoire de la ville de Québec 1608-1871,* Montréal and Ottawa, Boréal Express and Canadian Museum of Civilization, 1987, 399 pp.
A scholarly work, based on the evidence provided by French, British and Quebec archives. The writers take a fresh and exemplarily professional look at the forces that have shaped Québec; they also describe the process by which the city grew and thrived over the course of three centuries since its founding by Champlain. Complete with an excellent bibliography.

HULBERT, François. *Essai de géopolitique urbaine régionale,* Montréal, Éditions du Méridien, 1989, 473 pp.
A magisterial study of the multitude of problems arising from the development of a historic city at the heart of an expanding municipal community. The author identifies the contending powers in the urban situation and demonstrates how their actions affect the city's daily existence. A useful guide to urban affairs, in the tradition of the work done by the urbanist and sociologist Jean Cimon.

JOINT AUTHORSHIP. *Québec: Passion d'hiver,* Québec, Musée du Québec et Société Québec 2002, 1994, 143 pp.
A study of Québec, the snow-draped city, illustrated by drawings, paintings, and by the work of early and contemporary photographers, that describes the joy of living in a wintry country. Published as part of the *Québec plein la vue* exhibition at the Musée du Québec – June 1 to August 23, 1994.

JOINT AUTHORSHIP. *La ville de Québec. Histoire municipale,* Québec, Société historique de Québec. 4 volumes:
François-Xavier Chouinard (Régime français), 1963, 116 pp.
Antoine Drolet (Régime anglais jusqu'à l'incorporation, 1759-1833), 1965, 144 pp.
Antoine Drolet (De l'incorporation à la Confédération, 1837-1867), 143 pp.
Joint authorship (De la Confédération à la Charte de 1929), 1983, 246 pp.
A clerk of the City of Québec, a librarian in the Québec Archives, and a team of historians pooled their expertise, their methodology and their enthusiasm to produce a wide-ranging survey documenting the evolution of Québec's municipal affairs.

LAHOUD, Pierre, PAULETTE, Claude and TREMBLAY, Michel. *Québec à ciel ouvert,* Montréal, Libre Expression, 1987
Aerial photographs are an exciting way to explore the urban network, the counterplay between open and closed spaces. Québec has always been a photographer's dream at ground level; from a bird's-eye-view, the city takes on a dramatically new perspective.

LEBEL, Jean-Marie and ROY, Alain. *Photographies de Gabor Szilasi. Québec 1900-2000. Le siècle d'une capitale,* Québec, Multimondes et Commission de la capitale nationale, 2000, 159 pp.
During the course of the 20th century, the "old capital" has metamorphosed into an entirely new, national capital. Two historians draw up an initial balance sheet, assessing the consequences of its evolution over the last 300 years in an innovative and relevant manner. A good way "to grasp how yesterday's legacy stacks up against the challenges of tomorrow."

LEMIEUX, Louis-Guy. *Un amour de ville. Une chronique de Québec,* Montréal, Les Éditions de l'Homme, 1994, 359 pp. (Foreword by Michel Lessard.)
A journalist with the Québec City daily, *Le Soleil,* Louis-Guy Lemieux selects from three years' worth of personal views that he published as a roving reporter in the "big village" he loves so much and where he has lived for 40 years.

LEMOINE, James MacPherson. *Quebec Past and Present, a History of Quebec 1608-1876,* Québec, A. Côté et Cie, 1876, 466 pp.
During the 19th century, a number of writers from Québec's English-speaking, bicultural community wrote about their passionate feelings for their city in scholarly and artistic publications – all set down in the literary and ideological tone of the period. Lemoine was one of the most prolific in this group, equally interested in history, the natural sciences and the lives of the great families. His book entitled *Maple Leaves* is still today one of the inexhaustible sources of information about the capital.

LESSARD, Michel. *Les Livernois, photographes,* Québec, Musée du Québec, 1987, 338 pp.
A volume of photographs, introduced by a comprehensive account of the House of Livernois, Québec's most important photographic studio. For 120 years, from 1854 to 1974, studio members exploited every possible angle from which to capture the capital on film. A handsome proof of the artistic portrayal of the "soul" of Québec.

LESSARD, Michel. *Québec, ville du patrimoine mondial. Images oubliées de la vie quotidienne, 1858-1914,* Montréal, Les Éditions de l'Homme, 1992, 255 pp.
A visual journey through Québec based on early photographic images, with supporting text from a professional historian passionately involved with the city as a tourist attraction.

NOPPEN, Luc *et al. Québec, trois siècles d'architecture,* Montréal, Libre Expression, 1979, 440 pp.
By any measurement, the most complete study of the architectural and urban development of the historic city, written by the outstanding building expert in Québec. Generously illustrated, the work is based solidly on 20 years of research.

PELLERIN, Gilles. *Québec. Des écrivains dans la ville,* Québec, L'instant même et Musée du Québec, 1995, 175 pp.
Thirty-three writers who were born, have lived and still live in Québec bear witness, each in their individual way, to their common love for the city. "Québec casts a tantalizing spell on writers, forever appealing to their imagination, just as she always knows how to attract visitors into coming back time and time again to one of America's and the French-speaking world's favourite places," writes the narrator-publisher Gilles Pellerin on the back cover of the book.

PORTER, John, et PRIOUL, Didier. *Québec plein la vue,* Québec, Musée du Québec et Les Publications du Québec, 1994, 299 pp.
A carefully documented and lavishly illustrated catalogue of the *Québec plein la vue* exhibition. The volume contains eloquent tributes from writers and artists to the "soul" of their beloved city. An accessible work that deserves a place on everyone's bookshelves.

ROUTHIER, Adolphe-Basile. *Quebec at the Dawn of the 20th Century,* The Montreal Printing & Publishing Co., Ltd., 1900, 400 pp.
A striking example of book production, complete with gilt edges, printed on glossy paper, lavishly illustrated and augmented by numerous photographs of Québec at the beginning of the 20th century and of the well-known people who lived there. Written in a poetic murmur, the book explores various aspects of the city, each commanding its own chapter: "Picturesque Quebec," "Monumental Quebec," "Legendary Quebec," "Historic Quebec," "Social Quebec," "Archeological Quebec" [with "Stones That Speak"], "The City of the Dead," "Levis," and, finally, "Quebec in the 20th Century," which provides a look at what lies ahead for the capital.

ROY, Pierre-Georges. *La ville de Québec sous le Régime français,* Québec, Imprimeur de la Reine, 1930, tome 1: 548 pp., tome 2: 519 pp.
Québec's first archivist was one of the historic city's busiest chroniclers. His brief articles were the first popular accounts of the capital's past. A rich and lively source of information.

CONTENTS

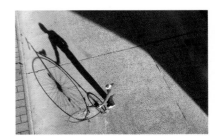

Lithographed on Jenson 200 M paper
and printed in Canada at Interglobe Printing Inc.
in March 2001.